LOW FAT COOKBOOK

Easy and delicious low-fat recipes

TABLE OF CONTENT

INTRODUCTION	4
Just hype or a healthy way to lose weight?!	4
What is the Low-Fat Diet anyway?	4
How do you follow the low-fat diet?	4
What are the benefits of the Low-Fat Diet?	5
Benefits of the Low-Fat Diet	6
LOW FAT RECIPES	7
ROAST VENISON	7
LIGHT TOMATO SOUP	8
LETSCHO	9
TROUT IN THE OVEN	11
ORIGINAL BOHEMIAN DUMPLINGS	12
ZUCCHINI SOUP	13
ASPARAGUS RISOTTO	14
VEGETARIAN SPAETZLE PAN	16
VEGETABLE RISOTTO	17
DONUTS FROM THE DONUT MAKER	18
CHINESE CABBAGE SALAD	20
RICE SALAD	21
CINNAMON PORRIDGE WITH BANANA	23
FRIED POTATOES FROM THE AIR FRYER	24
OATMEAL SOUP	25
QUICK SALMON FILLET	26
ZUCCHINI SOUP	27
GRANDMA'S BOILED BEEF	28
RUMPSTEAK	30
CHILI SIN CARNE	31
RICE SOUP	32
CABBAGE SOUP FOR DETOX	33
SIMPLE CHIVE SAUCE	35
POTATOES FROM THE STEAMER	36
WRAPS WITH VEGETABLES	37

CELERY PUREE	38
KOHLRABI SALAD WITH APPLES	39
JUICY BEIRIED	40
MUSHROOM RISOTTO	42
TOMATO SALAD	43
BURNED-IN LENSES	44
FLUFF	45
PUMPKIN SPAETZLE	47
FRIED PIKEPERCH WITH GARLIC	48
MANGO CHUTNEY	49
ICEBERG LETTUCE WITH YOGURT	50
IRISH STEW	51
PUT IN CHILI PEPPERS	53
COLESLAW	54
CARROT MUFFINS	55
PUMPKIN SLICE	56
ZUCCHINI CHIPS	58
TOMATO PASTE	59
POTATO CHEESE	60
APPLE HORSERADISH	61
MILLET	62
TROUT MILLER	63
CHIVES AND EGGS SPREAD	64
VIENNESE PASTA SALAD	65
WRAPS WITH SALMON	67

INTRODUCTION
Just hype or a healthy way to lose weight?!

How was that? Fat makes you fat? The 80s are back, because at that time, Low Fat was THE diet to lose weight! Although low carb trend of recent years, but Low Fat holds adamantly. You can find out everything you should know about a low-fat diet here!

What is the Low-Fat Diet anyway?

The low-fat diet is - oh wonder - about saving fat as much as possible! After all, fat is the macronutrient with the most calories. As a reminder: protein and carbohydrates provide you with 4 calories per gram, fat more than double that with 9 calories per gram. And if you save this energy, then your calorie balance should go into the red more easily. But you shouldn't cut the fat entirely, which is also quite difficult, as many protein-rich foods also contain fat at the same time. In addition, your body relies on a certain amount of fat and if you completely do without it, then it does you much more harm than that Low fat diet brings something. Plus, fat isn't bad per se!

How do you follow the low-fat diet?

The low-fat diet is less of one of the numerous crash diets, but more of a way of eating. Besides, she really doesn't have any specific rules other than saving fat.

While you are following the low-fat diet, your fat intake should only account for 10% to a maximum of 30% of your daily energy intake. Depending on your personal macro distribution, that can be as little as 30 grams of fat per day. So "simply" avoid high-fat foods and pay attention to the low daily amount of fat. In return, you can eat more carbohydrates and proteins. But please watch out for complex carbs and not much more protein than you normally eat. And while we're at it: When choosing the few fats that you are allowed to eat, pay attention to healthy fats.

To go with it: carbohydrates for weight loss.

For information: The German Nutrition Society recommends getting around 25-30% of the total daily calories from fats for a balanced and healthy diet - 7-10% each from polyunsaturated, monounsaturated and also saturated. Trans fats should only make up a maximum of 1% of the daily food energy. All in all, that would add up to 60-80 grams of fat. So, you save quite a bit of fat through a low-fat diet.

What are the benefits of the Low-Fat Diet?

As I said, the low-fat diet should help you save calories more easily. Because the less energy-rich macros you eat, the better your calorie balance is. In order to know how much you are "allowed" to eat, you should first calculate your calorie requirement and know how high or low your basal metabolic rate and your performance metabolic rate are.

Some of you may find it easier to lose weight on a low-fat diet because you can eat carbs and avoid cravings. Eliminating fat is often easier for the body than avoiding carbs. In addition, your body uses the high-carb-low-fat diet for the energy it needs. If you then eat enough protein, your body uses everything directly to maintain and build muscle mass. More muscle mass, in turn, requires more energy - you lose weight even better.

Which foods are allowed in the low-fat diet and which are not?

For the most part, your low-fat diet should include low-fat foods like these:

Fresh fruits and vegetables

Low fat fish

Low-fat meat

Low fat dairy products

Complex carbohydrates such as whole grain pasta, potatoes, rice, whole grain bread, quinoa

legumes

Have a look in the recipe area. There you will definitely find some delicious low-fat recipes and meals that stimulate fat burning.

You should avoid this in the low-fat nutrition plan or only consume it very little:

- nuts
- avocado
- Oils
- Butter, margarine

High-fat dairy products such as yoghurts, cream, cheese and the like, all recognizable by their cream levels or fat i. T.

Oily fish like mackerel

Fatty meat like bacon

Attention: Please pay attention to the list of ingredients for special low-fat products, because if fat is missing, something else - often sugar - is often represented in larger quantities. So don't be lulled by all the advertising frenzy. The bottom line is that you may be consuming even more calories than if you were to eat the "normal" version of the product. Not through fat, but through simple carbs. If it says "low in fat", it doesn't have to mean "low in calories".

Benefits of the Low-Fat Diet

- Easy to implement as there are no specific rules
- You will consume fewer calories if you do not completely replenish the deficit with the other macros
- Cholesterol levels can improve
- No cravings due to lack of carbs
- Lower risk of cardiovascular disease and arteriosclerosis

LOW FAT RECIPES
ROAST VENISON

Ingredients for 4 servings

- 800　　G　　Roe deer
- 2　　　Pc　　onion
- Soup greens (vegetables)
- 250　　ml　　red wine
- 3rd　　Tbsp　Tomato paste
- 2　　　Tbsp　Bona olive oil
- 1　　　prize　salt
- 1　　　prize　pepper

time

105 min. Total time 15 min preparation time 90 min. cooking & resting time

preparation

First cut the soup vegetables into cubes.

Now rub the roe deer with salt and pepper. Heat the oil in a pan and sear the Schlögel on all sides. Remove the meat from the pan and set aside, deglaze the meat stock with red wine and bring to the boil.

Pour some oil into a roasting pan. Add the vegetables and the meat stock. Stir in tomato paste and add the meat.

Now slowly braise the roast venison in the preheated oven at 160 ° C for about 1.5 hours. Constantly pour liquid over meat.

Then cut open and serve with the juice.

LIGHT TOMATO SOUP

Ingredients for 4 servings

- 600 ml Soup (or soup cubes)
- 1 kg Fully ripe tomatoes
- 1 branch thyme
- 4th Bl basil
- 2 Tbsp Cream with little fat content (whipped)
- 1 Pc clove of garlic
- 30th ml Bona olive oil
- 1 prize pepper
- 1 prize salt
- 100 ml Cream (light with little fat)
- 80 G Finely chopped onion

time

30 min. Total time 20 min preparation time 10 min.cooking & resting time

preparation

For the light tomato soup, heat the olive oil in a saucepan, add the onion and finely chopped garlic and sauté until translucent.

Quarter the washed tomatoes and then add to the saucepan with the sprig of thyme and basil leaves. Pour the soup on top and season everything with salt and pepper. Simmer the tomato soup for about 10 minutes.

Then mix the soup, pass through a fine sieve and refine with the liquid cream.

Arrange the soup in plates and garnish with a topping and a basil leaf.

LETSCHO

Ingredients for 6 servings

- 500 G tomato
- 500 G paprika
- 3rd Pc onion
- 1 shot Bona oil
- 1 Tbsp Paprika powder, mild

- 1 prize salt
- 1 TL sugar
- 1 prize pepper from the grinder
- 2 Tbsp Ketchup
- 2 Pc clove of garlic
- 1 TL Paprika, schraf
- 150 ml water

time

30 min. Total time 15 min preparation time 15 min.cooking & resting time

preparation

For the homemade letscho, peel and chop the onion and garlic.

Wash, core and stem the peppers and cut into bite-sized pieces.

Wash the tomatoes, with hot water blanch , remove the skin and cut into small cubes also.

Then brown the onion and garlic pieces in a saucepan with oil or butter until translucent.

Then add the pepper and tomato cubes as well as a little ketchup, stir well and fill up with a dash of water.

Season to taste with salt, pepper, sugar and paprika powder.

Bring the vegetables to the boil and then simmer / simmer for about 20-25 minutes until they are soft - stirring occasionally.

TROUT IN THE OVEN

Ingredients for 2 servings

- 2   Pc   Trout
- 1   TL   salt
- 2   Tbsp   Bona olive oil
- 4th   branch thyme
- 4th   branch rosemary
- 4th   branch parsley

time

25 min. Total time 10 min preparation time 15 min.cooking & resting time

preparation

For trout in the oven, of course, the oven must be preheated to 240 degrees. Wash and drain herbs.

Rinse the trout under running water, drain gently. Season the inside and outside with salt and rub with oil. Put sprigs of thyme, sprigs of rosemary and parsley in the trout's abdominal cavity.

Now place the fish on a baking sheet lined with baking paper (or in an aluminum cup) and roast in the oven for about 10 to 15 minutes.

ORIGINAL BOHEMIAN DUMPLINGS

Ingredients for 10 servings

- 2   Pc   Eggs
- 1   Wf   yeast
- 500   ml   lukewarm milk or water
- 1   kg   Flour
- 2   TL   salt
- 1   TL   sugar

time

95 min. Total time 15 min preparation time 80 min.cooking & resting time

preparation

Put the flour and salt in a bowl. Dissolve the yeast with the sugar in the milk by stirring everything well with a spoon, then let stand until the dough starts to bubble. Then add the mixture to the flour. Add the eggs and knead the dough well until it becomes nice and smooth.

It can't be too watery or too dry. If necessary, add a little more flour or water. The right dough looks nice and smooth and does not stick to the bowl. If the dough is prepared correctly, it will be filled with lots of tiny air bubbles.

Let the dough rise three times for 20 minutes at room temperature. Each time it rises, knead the dough again briefly and let it rise again.

Use a knife to cut the dough into three equal parts and form long rolls from them.

In a large (possibly oblong) saucepan, salt the water and bring to the boil. Put in the long rolls and cook for 20 to 25 minutes, depending on their size. From time to time to turn. It is necessary to use a large saucepan as the dough will rise. Turn down the temperature. The dumpling should steep in the flowing water, not boil too much.

Cut the finished dumplings into slices while still hot with the help of a thread. You can also use a dumpling cutter if you have one.

ZUCCHINI SOUP

Ingredients for 4 servings

- 1   Pc   onion
- 400   G   zucchini
- 2   Tbsp   Bona oil
- 0.75   l   vegetable soup
- 0.06   l   milk
- 1   prize   pepper
- 1   prize   salt

time

30 min. Total time 15 min preparation time 15 min.cooking & resting time

preparation

Peel and chop the onion. Wash and clean the zucchini and cut into large cubes.

Roast the onion in a saucepan with oil, add the zucchini, roast briefly and then add the soup. Let the soup cook on a low flame for about 15 minutes.

Puree the soup with the blender. Then add the milk, season with salt and pepper and stir again until creamy with the blender.

ASPARAGUS RISOTTO

Ingredients for 4 servings

- 250 G Risotto rice
- 400 G Asparagus (green)
- 800 ml Asparagus stock
- 1 Pc onion

- 40 G butter
- 1 prize salt
- 1 prize pepper
- 1 shot Bona oil
- 1 shot White wine
- 80 G Parmesan

time

20 min. Total time 10 min preparation time 10 min.cooking & resting time

preparation

For the delicious asparagus risotto, peel the asparagus and cut off the woody ends. Boil the tips in salted water until they are firm to the bite. Carefully remove the asparagus pieces from the asparagus stock. Then quench with cold water. Cut the cooked asparagus into medium-sized pieces. Save asparagus stock!

Finely dice the onion. Put the olive oil in a saucepan, let it get hot and fry the onion briefly. Add the rice, fry briefly, pour in the asparagus stock, simmer the rice in it until it is firm to the bite, season with salt. Stir frequently at the same time.

Then add the asparagus slices. Fold in the butter and parmesan and season with salt.

VEGETARIAN SPAETZLE PAN

Ingredients for 2 servings

- 2   Tbsp   butter
- 160   G   leek
- 3rd   Pc   Carrots (medium)
- 2   Pc   zucchini
- 500   G   Spaetzle (cooling shelf)
- 100   ml   Soup (clear)
- 80   G   Cheese (grated)
- 1   prize   pepper
- 1   prize   salt

time

30 min. Total time 15 min preparation time 15 min.cooking & resting time

preparation

For the vegetarian spaetzle pan, first wash the leek and cut into rings. Peel and roughly grate the carrots. Wash and clean the zucchini and cut into strips.

Sear the vegetables and spaetzle in a pan with butter and deglaze with the soup.

Let simmer briefly, mix in the cheese and season with salt and pepper.

VEGETABLE RISOTTO

Ingredients for 4 servings

- 300 G Risotto rice
- 0.5 l Vegetable soup (clear)
- 1 Can Corn
- 400 G tomatoes
- 1 Pc zucchini
- 3rd Pc Carrots
- 1 Pc onion
- 3rd Tbsp Bona oil
- 35 G Cheese (e.g. parmesan)
- 1 prize pepper
- 1 prize salt

time

35 min. Total time 15 min preparation time 20 min.cooking & resting time

preparation

For the risotto, first prepare the clear vegetable soup according to the basic recipe. Chop the onion into small pieces. Briefly sauté risotto rice with oil and onion in a large saucepan.

Pour the risotto with the soup and let it simmer. Always add a little and only pour in when everything is over cooked. Repeat until the rice is ready.

Meanwhile, sieve the corn, finely dice the tomatoes, peel the carrots and chop finely. Also cut the zucchini and discard the ends.

Briefly fry the vegetables separately in a pan with a little oil and then add to the risotto.

Season to taste with salt, pepper and possibly spices such as oregano. Finally, sprinkle with cheese as desired.

DONUTS FROM THE DONUT MAKER

Ingredients for 6 servings

- 260 G Flour
- 1 Pk Vanilla sugar
- 1 prize salt
- 3rd Pc Eggs
- 1 Pk baking powder

- 50 ml Bona oil
- 250 ml milk
- 130 G Icing sugar

time

25 min. Total time 25 min preparation time

preparation

Sift the flour into a bowl and mix with the baking powder. Add icing sugar, vanilla sugar, milk, eggs, oil and salt and work into a smooth dough.

Heat the donut maker and brush with a little oil. Pour approx. 1 tablespoon of dough each into the indentations provided. Close the device and bake the donuts for about 3-4 minutes. Continue like this until all of the batter is used.

Sprinkle the donuts with icing sugar.

CHINESE CABBAGE SALAD

A recipe for Chinese cabbage salad is very popular in the cold season. It goes well with various types of meat as a side dish.

Chinese cabbage salad

Ingredients for 2 servings

- 1 Pc Chinese cabbage
- 1 prize Pepper (colored, freshly ground)

Ingredients for the salad marinade

- 1 TL salt
- 220 ml water
- 1 Tbsp Bona oil
- 2 TL Granulated sugar
- 2 Tbsp vinegar

time

15 min. Total time 15 min preparation time

preparation

Remove the outer leaves of the Chinese cabbage. Remove the remaining leaves from the stalk and wash under running water.

Now cut the leaves into fine, thin strips and place in a salad bowl.

Refine with a popular salad marinade made from water, salt, sugar, oil and vinegar and season with freshly ground pepper if necessary.

RICE SALAD

Ingredients for 6 servings

- 300   G   Long grain rice
- 80   G   Peas, fresh or frozen
- 3rd   Pc   Spring onions, in rings
- 1   Pc   green peppers, finely diced
- 1   Pc   red peppers, finely diced
- 300   G   Canned corn kernels
- 15th   G   Mint, crushed

Ingredients for the dressing

- 1   Pc   Clove of garlic (crushed)
- 125   ml   Bona olive oil
- 2   Tbsp   Lemon juice
- 1   TL   sugar
- 1   prize   pepper
- 1   prize   salt

time

50 min. Total time 30 min preparation time 20 min.cooking & resting time

preparation

For the rice salad, bring the water to the boil in a large saucepan and stir in the rice. Bring to the boil and simmer for 12-15 minutes, until the rice is firm to the bite. Drain and let cool.

Boil the peas for approx. 2 minutes in a small saucepan with boiling water. Rinse under cold water and drain well.

For the dressing, mix the oil, lemon juice, garlic and sugar in a small mixing bowl and whisk well. Season to taste with salt and freshly ground black pepper.

Put the rice, peas, spring onions, bell pepper, corn, and mint in a large bowl. Add the dressing and mix well. Cover and put in the fridge for 1 hour. Then transfer to a salad bowl.

CINNAMON PORRIDGE WITH BANANA

Ingredients for 2 servings

- 35 G oatmeal
- 200 ml milk
- 1 prize cinnamon
- 2 Tbsp sugar
- 1 Pc banana

time

20 min. Total time 20 min preparation time

preparation

Simmer the oatmeal, milk, sugar and cinnamon in a small saucepan for 5 minutes, stirring constantly, until the porridge has the right consistency. Cut the banana into pieces and mash it in the pulp. Let cool and serve or take away.

FRIED POTATOES FROM THE AIR FRYER

Ingredients for 2 servings

- 2   Pc   big potato
- 1   Tbsp   Bona oil
- 1   prize   oregano
- 1   prize   Caraway seed
- 1   prize   thyme
- 1   prize   salt

time

25 min. Total time 10 min preparation time 15 min.cooking & resting time

preparation

Peel the potato and cut into 1 cm wide slices. Mix the spices, pour over the potato slices, add oil and mix everything well.

Put in the air fryer, deep-fry for 7 minutes at 180 °, shake and deep-fry for another 7 minutes.

OATMEAL SOUP

Ingredients for 2 servings

- 1   Pc   egg
- 2   Tbsp   butter
- 5   Tbsp   oatmeal
- 1   prize   salt
- 1   prize   pepper
- 1   Pc   carrot
- 0.5 l   vegetable soup

time

20 min. Total time 5 min preparation time 15 min.cooking & resting time

preparation

Melt the butter in a saucepan and brown the oat flakes in it until golden. Deglaze with the vegetable soup and bring to the boil.

Grate or finely chop the carrots and add. Whisk and stir in the egg. Let simmer for about 15 minutes, until the oat flakes and carrots are soft. Season to taste with salt and pepper.

QUICK SALMON FILLET

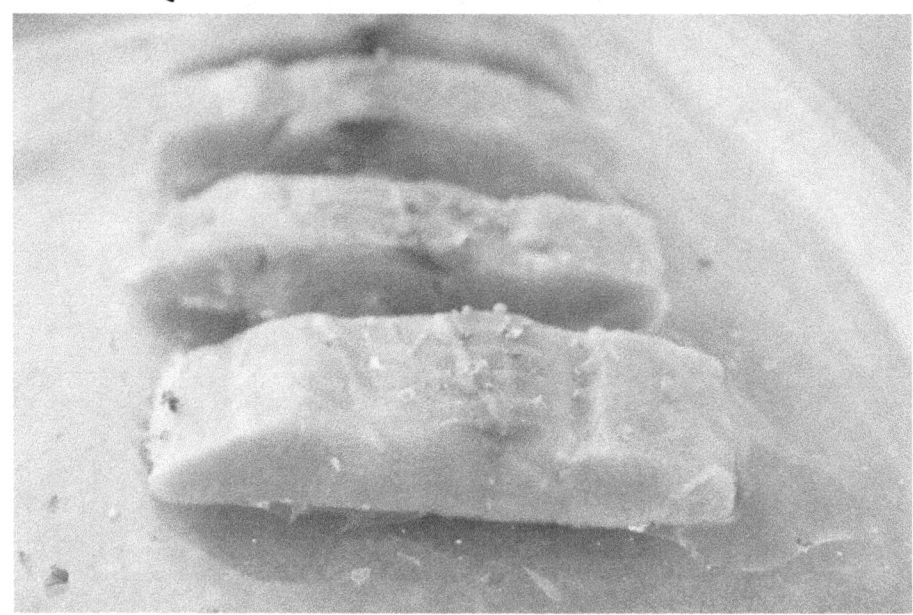

Ingredients for 4 servings

- 800   G   Salmon fillet
- 4th   Tbsp   Bona olive oil
- 1   shot   Bona olive oil
- 1   prize   salt
- 1   prize   pepper
- 2   Tbsp   Lemon juice

time

10 min. Total time 10 min preparation time

preparation

The oven is preheated to 250 ° C.

The salmon fillet is then deboned and cut into fine slices about 1 cm thick.

A baking sheet is brushed vigorously with olive oil and then the slices are placed on it. Now the salmon is seasoned with salt, pepper and lemon juice as desired and everything is drizzled with 4 tablespoons of olive oil

Finally, the baking sheet is placed in the hot oven and cooked for only 4 minutes.

ZUCCHINI SOUP

Ingredients for 4 servings

- 3rd   Pc   Zucchini (medium)
- 1   Pc   onion
- 4th   Pc   Garlic cloves
- 1   prize   salt
- 1   prize   pepper
- 0.5   l   water
- 20th   G   butter
- 1   prize   Nutmeg
- 1   Federation parsley

time

30 min. Total time 15 min preparation time 15 min.cooking & resting time

preparation

Wash the zucchini well under lukewarm water.

Remove both ends of the zucchini. Then dice the zucchini. To do this, cut them lengthways once so that you get two halves and then cut them into small pieces and put them in a bowl.

Peel the onion. Now you dice the onion, that is, you cut it as small as possible. Do the same with 4 cloves of garlic. You can use just two toes to suit your taste.

Now add a little butter, i.e. 1 cut about half a centimeter thick, into the pan and wait until it starts to bubble slightly.

Now put the garlic and the onion in the pan and let it fry a little - stir it again and again so that nothing burns.

Now add the zucchini pieces from the bowl. Let them sear briefly as well. Don't forget - always stir so that nothing burns.

After a few minutes, the zucchini pieces should have a little color, transfer the whole thing into a saucepan and add half a liter of warm water (more if necessary). Let everything simmer for about 15 minutes.

Now chop a bunch of parsley, that is, as small as possible again, and add it to the soup.

Season to taste with a little salt, pepper and nutmeg as required.

When the zucchini are soft after about 15 minutes, puree the soup to the desired consistency (one person likes his soup thicker, the other thinner) and you are ready to serve.

GRANDMA'S BOILED BEEF

Ingredients for 6 servings

- 1 TL salt
- 1 Msp nutmeg
- 5 Pc Bay leaves

- 1   Tbsp   Peppercorns
- 1   Pc   onion
- 2   Cup   Soup greens
- 1   kg   Beef bones
- 2   kg   Table splash

time

165 min. Total time 15 min preparation time 150 min.cooking & resting time

preparation

Peel and halve the onion and roast the cut surface until dark.

Wash the boiled beef and beef bones with cold water. Bring about 5 liters of water to a boil in a large saucepan. Put in boiled beef, bones, peppercorns and bay leaves, boil gently and simmer and skim off the foam again and again.

After about 1.5 hours add the vegetables and the onion halves. Let everything simmer gently for another hour. Lift the cooked, crumbly meat out of the pot, season the soup with salt, pepper and nutmeg and strain through a sieve.

These apple horseradish serve.

RUMPSTEAK

Ingredients for 4 servings

- 4th   Schb   Rump steaks a 200g (well hung)
- 2   Tbsp   Coconut oil
- 1   Cup   Pepper, freshly ground
- 1   TL   Steak seasoning

time

15 min. Total time 7 min preparation time 8 min.cooking & resting time

preparation

Take the meat slices out of the refrigerator at least 10 minutes before use. Preheat the oven to 100 degrees upper and lower heating. Slide a wire shelf in the middle.

Let the coconut oil get really hot in the pan. Pat the meat slices dry and fry for 2 minutes on each side (turn only once).

Take the steaks out of the pan and place them on the wire shelf in the oven. Cook for 8 minutes. Take out and sprinkle with steak seasoning and grind with pepper.

CHILI SIN CARNE

Ingredients for 4 servings

- 400 G Carrots
- 1 Pc Onion (medium)
- 1 Pc clove of garlic
- 300 G Kidney beans (can)
- 200 G Corn (can)
- 1 Pc Paprika (red or green)
- 60 G Celery (or celery)
- 2 Tbsp Tomato paste
- 400 G tomatoes
- 1 shot Bona oil
- 200 ml Vegetable soup (clear)
- 1 Pc Chilli pepper (red)
- 0.5 Federation Parsley (fresh)
- 1 prize Cayenne pepper
- 1 prize salt

time

60 min. Total time 40 min preparation time 20 min.cooking & resting time

preparation

For the Chili Sin Carne, peel the carrots with a peeler and cut into small cubes. Peel onion and garlic and chop finely. Remove the beans and corn from the can, rinse with clean water and drain.

Wash the peppers, cut into pods and then dice the pods. Wash the celery, finely trim the edges, cut the rest into small cubes. Wash tomatoes and cut into small cubes.

Now heat the oil in a saucepan, first roast the onion with the garlic until golden. Add the carrots, paprika and celery and let sweat briefly while stirring. Add tomatoes. Pour soup on top. Finally add the tomato paste and simmer gently on a low flame for about 20 minutes.

Meanwhile, finely chop the parsley and fresh chilli. Just before the end of the cooking time, add the beans, corn, parsley and chilli to the dish. Also season with salt and cayenne pepper to taste. Refine with parsley.

RICE SOUP

Ingredients for 4 servings

- 1.25 l Vegetable broth
- 1 prize salt
- 0.5 Federation chives
- 50 G rice
- 1 Pc egg

time

30 min. Total time 10 min preparation time 20 min.cooking & resting time

preparation

Wash the rice thoroughly. Bring the broth to a boil and stir in the rice.

Cook over a moderate heat for about 20 minutes, do not cover and stir every now and then. At the end of the cooking time, season with salt.

Wash the chives and cut into rolls with the scissors. Stir the egg into the soup and sprinkle with chives

CABBAGE SOUP FOR DETOX

Ingredients for 4 servings

- 0.5 Pc herb

- 3rd   Pc   onion
- 1   Pc   celery
- 2   Pc   paprika
- 4th   Pc   tomatoes
- 2   Pc   Carrots
- 1.5   l   Vegetable soup (basic)
- 1   prize   pepper
- 1   TL   curry
- 1   Federation   parsley

time

50 min. Total time 20 min preparation time 30 min.cooking & resting time

preparation

They only use fresh ingredients for the cabbage soup to detox. First clean the cabbage, remove the stalk and cut finely. Wash and drain well. Peel and chop the onions.

Clean and wash tomatoes, peppers, carrots and celery and cut into pieces.

Put everything in a saucepan with the soup and cook the vegetables until soft. Season to taste with pepper and curry.

Just before serving, wash the parsley, chop it finely and stir it into the soup.

SIMPLE CHIVE SAUCE

Ingredients for 4 servings

- 1   cups   yogurt
- 1   cups   Schärdinger Berghof sour cream
- 1   prize   sugar
- 0.5 TL   salt
- 1   prize   Pepper from the grinder)
- 1   Federation   chives

time

15 min. Total time 15 min preparation time

preparation

For the simple chive sauce, first mix the yogurt, sour cream, salt, pepper and sugar in a bowl.

Wash the chives, drain them and cut into fine rolls. Stir into the sauce and serve.

POTATOES FROM THE STEAMER

Ingredients for 4 servings

- 1	kg	Potatoes
- 1	prize	salt

time

45 min. Total time 10 min preparation time 35 min.cooking & resting time

preparation

Peel and dice the potatoes and place in the perforated steamer. Season with salt and bay leaf and steam for approx. 15 minutes.

Excellent as a side dish and quickly prepared in the steamer.

WRAPS WITH VEGETABLES

Ingredients for 4 servings

- 0.5　Stg　leek
- 1　prize　pepper
- 1　Pk　cress
- 4th　Pc　Lettuce leaves
- 4th　Pc　wraps
- 0.5　Pk　cream cheese
- 0.5　cups　yogurt
- 1　Can　Corn
- 3rd　Pc　tomatoes
- 1　Pc　cucumber
- 1　prize　salt

time

20 min. Total time 20 min preparation time

preparation

For the wraps with vegetables, first wash the leek and cut into rings. Wash and chop the cucumber, wash the tomatoes and also cut into small pieces. Drain the corn well in a sieve.

Now mix the prepared vegetables well in a bowl with yogurt, cheese, salt and pepper. Wash the cress and lettuce leaves well and drain well.

Now cover the wraps with a lettuce leaf, spread the vegetable mixture on top and sprinkle with cress. Roll up the wraps and serve.

CELERY PUREE

Ingredients for 3 servings

- 1   Pc   onion
- 3rd Pc   Garlic cloves
- 2   Tbsp   Bona oil
- 1   Pc   celery
- 1   prize salt
- 1   prize Pepper from the grinder)
- 1   Msp   nutmeg
- 0.25 l   Soup

time

40 min. Total time 20 min preparation time 20 min.cooking & resting time

preparation

For the celery puree, first peel the onion and garlic and sauté in a saucepan with oil.

Peel and dice the celery bulb as well. Add to the pot and sauté briefly. Now deglaze with some soup and steam the vegetables until soft.

Then drain the soup and puree the vegetables with the hand blender. Season with salt, pepper and nutmeg.

KOHLRABI SALAD WITH APPLES

Ingredients for 4 servings

- 0.5   cups   Schärdinger Berghof sour cream
- 1   Pc   onion
- 0.5   Federation   parsley
- 1   Pc   Lemons (juice)

- 1   Tbsp   honey
- 800   G   Kohlrabi
- 2   Pc   Apples
- 1   prize pepper
- 1   prize salt

time

15 min. Total time 15 min preparation time

preparation

Peel the apples and kohlrabi and grate finely. Peel onions and cut them into fine pieces.

Wash, drain and chop the parsley.

Mix lemon juice, honey, salt, pepper and sour cream into a dressing.

Pour the sauce over the salad and mix well.

JUICY BEIRIED

Ingredients for 6 servings

- 1 kg Advisory
- 1 Federation Soup vegetables
- 1 Pc carrot
- 1.5 Pc Onions
- 1 Tbsp Schärdinger Berghof sour cream
- 2 Tbsp Bona oil
- 5 Pc Capers
- 1 Wf sugar
- 1 TL mustard
- 1 TL salt
- 0.5 TL pepper
- 1 shot vinegar

time

110 min. Total time 20 min preparation time 90 min.cooking & resting time

preparation

For the juicy beiried - it is also known as roast beef or ribs - first wash or peel the carrots, roots and onions, cut into small pieces and briefly toast in a pan with olive oil and sugar. Deglaze with a dash of vinegar and season with salt.

Now sear the beetroot in this pan on all sides and pour warm water over it until everything is covered - let it simmer for about an hour and a half (simmer).

Then remove the meat from the braised juice and keep it warm. Strain the braised juice through a sieve. Season the whole thing with mustard, pepper and capers and thicken with sour cream and, if necessary, with a little flour.

MUSHROOM RISOTTO

Ingredients for 4 servings

- 1 prize salt
- 1 prize pepper
- 1 Pc clove of garlic
- 1 Tbsp chopped parsley
- 1 Pc Red onion
- 100 G grated parmesan
- 150 ml White wine
- 300 G Risotto rice
- 350 ml vegetable soup
- 2 Tbsp Bona olive oil
- 250 G Mushrooms of your choice
- 1 Stg Leek (cut)

time

25 min. Total time 5 min preparation time 20 min.cooking & resting time

preparation

Pour the risotto rice, white wine and vegetable soup into an unperforated cooking bowl and cook in the steamer at 100 ° C for about 16 minutes.

Chop the onion, clean the mushrooms and finely slice them. Sauté together with the parsley and the chopped leek in a pan with olive oil. Add the pressed garlic and sauté briefly.

Stir the mushroom mixture into the risotto and cook for another 4 minutes. If necessary, add a little vegetable soup.

Finally add the grated Parmesan and season the risotto with salt and pepper.

TOMATO SALAD

Ingredients for 1 serving

- 1   Tbsp   basil
- 3rd   Tbsp   Bona olive oil
- 1   prize   salt
- 3rd   Pc   tomatoes
- 1   Pc   onion
- 1   shot   Lemon juice
- 1   shot   vinegar
- 1   prize   sugar

time

10 min. Total time 10 min preparation time

preparation

Cut tomatoes into slices (or wedges). Peel the onion, cut into cubes and add to the tomatoes with the finely chopped basil.

Then add the olive oil, a dash of vinegar, lemon juice and a pinch of sugar, mix well and season with salt.

BURNED-IN LENSES

Ingredients for 4 servings

- 1 Can Lentils (large, 480 g)
- 2 Pc Onion (finely chopped)
- 200 G Bacon cubes
- 4th Tbsp Flour smooth)
- 2 Pc Clove of garlic (finely chopped)
- 1 prize marjoram
- 1 Pc Bay leaf

- 1   Pc   Soup cubes
- 1   shot   vinegar
- 0.5 l   water

time

40 min. Total time 15 min preparation time 25 min.cooking & resting time

preparation

Strain the lenses (collect the lens fluid). Leave the bacon cubes in a pan over a mild heat and brown a little - remove the bacon from the pan.

Fry the onion in the same pan until it is lightly browned, then add the garlic and fry briefly. Add the flour and stir-fry until lightly browned.

Pour in the lentil water and 1/2 liter of water, season with the soup cube, add the bay leaf, marjoram, bacon cubes and the lentils.

Cover and simmer the lentils gently for 15-25 minutes, after the end of the cooking time season the lentils again with salt / pepper / vinegar.

FLUFF

Ingredients for 4 servings

- 500   G   Veal lung

- 1 Pc Veal heart
- 1 Federation Root system (carrot, celery)
- 1 Pc Bay leaf
- 4th Pc Juniper berries
- 5 Pc Peppercorns
- 1 Pc onion
- 1 prize salt
- 1 prize thyme
- 1 shot Lemon juice

Ingredients for the sauce

- 40 G butter
- 40 G Flour
- 1 Pc Onion (small)
- 1 Pc clove of garlic
- 1 Pc Lemon (peel, untreated)
- 1 prize Parsley (freshly chopped)
- 1 shot vinegar
- 1 prize sugar
- 3rd Tbsp Schärdinger Berghof sour cream
- 3rd Tbsp Whipped cream
- 1 prize salt
- 1 prize pepper

time

60 min. Total time 20 min preparation time 40 min. cooking & resting time

preparation

Wash the roots (carrots, celery, yellow turnips, etc.) and cut into pieces. Wash your lungs and heart.

Let the oil get hot in a large saucepan. Briefly fry the roots in it and pour 2.5-3 liters of water, season with salt. Add bay leaf, peppercorns, juniper berries, thyme, whole onion, whole clove of garlic, lung and heart and simmer over low heat for approx. 40 min.

After approx. 25 minutes, take the lungs out of the water and put them briefly in cold water. Let the heart continue to boil. Then remove the heart and let it cool down over water.

Cut the heart and fluff into fine strips. Mix with salt, pepper and lemon juice and set aside.

For the sauce: finely chop the onion and parsley, place in a bowl with the lemon zest and marjoram. Let the butter get hot in a pan and toast the flour in it. Add the anchovy mixture and briefly toast. Pour over the vinegar and water. Let the sauce simmer for approx. 15-20 minutes, stir frequently.

Add the sliced Beuschl, add the whipped cream, stir. Season to taste with spices.

The Beuschel is served with bread dumplings and green salad.

PUMPKIN SPAETZLE

Ingredients for 4 servings

- 2   Pc   Eggs
- 100   G   wheat flour
- 100   G   Spelled flour
- 100   G   pumpkin
- 1   prize   salt
- 1   prize   nutmeg
- 2   Tbsp   butter
- 50   ml   milk

time

30 min. Total time 10 min preparation time 20 min.cooking & resting time

preparation

Whisk eggs and milk, add flour, season with salt and nutmeg.

Peel and finely grate the pumpkin, add to the batter and stir well. (If the mixture is too runny, use more flour, if the mixture is too firm, add more milk or a dash of water.)

Bring the water to the boil with a little salt. Press the mixture through a spaetzle sieve, bring to the boil briefly and rinse in cold water. Sieve the spaetzle and toss in a pan with melted butter.

FRIED PIKEPERCH WITH GARLIC

Ingredients for 4 servings

- 4th   Pc   Pikeperch fillets
- 0.5   Pc   Lemon juice from it
- 2   Tbsp   butter
- 2   prize   salt

- 3rd   Pc   Garlic cloves
- 1   prize   pepper

time

25 min. Total time 10 min preparation time 15 min.cooking & resting time

preparation

For the fried pikeperch with garlic, first season the fish fillet with salt, pepper and lemon juice.

Chop the garlic into fine pieces and fry some of it in a pan in hot butter. Briefly fry the pikeperch fillets in the garlic butter on both sides.

Add the remaining garlic to the fish shortly before the end of the cooking time and then let the fillets simmer for a few minutes.

MANGO CHUTNEY

Ingredients for 4 servings

- 2   Pc   onion
- 3rd   Pc   Mangoes (medium)
- 2   Tbsp   sugar
- 180   ml   Balsamic vinegar

- 0.5   TL   Chili powder
- 100   ml   water
- 1   prize pepper
- 1   prize salt

time

45 min. Total time 20 min preparation time 25 min.cooking & resting time

preparation

Finely chop the onion. Peel the mangoes and cut into fine strips.

Heat the water and sugar and let them caramelize. Now add the onion and cook for 2-3 minutes. Then pour the vinegar on top and let it stew for another 5 minutes.

Add the mango strips and let them simmer for approx. 25 minutes until it has a thick consistency.

Season with salt, pepper and chili powder and pour into clean preserving jars. Immediately close the jars and place on the lid, leave to cool.

ICEBERG LETTUCE WITH YOGURT

Ingredients for 4 servings

- 1 cups yogurt
- 1 Pc Iceberg lettuce
- 2 Tbsp Lemon juice
- 2 Tbsp Bona olive oil
- 1 prize sugar
- 1 prize pepper
- 1 prize salt

time

15 min. Total time 15 min preparation time

preparation

Divide the lettuce, pluck into bite-sized pieces and then wash well. Drain.

For the dressing, mix the remaining ingredients well in a bowl.

Mix the dressing well with the salad.

IRISH STEW

Ingredients for 4 servings

- 1   kg   Lamb shoulder
- 800   G   White cabbage
- 4th   Pc   onion
- 4th   Pc   Garlic cloves
- 2   Tbsp   Caraway seed
- 1   TL   salt
- 1   TL   pepper
- 400   G   Carrots
- 350   G   Potatoes
- 1   Federation   parsley
- 900   ml   Meatsoup
- 100   G   Bacon, streaky

time

40 min. Total time 15 min preparation time 25 min.cooking & resting time

preparation

For the Irish stew, first cut the lamb into bite-sized cubes. Peel and roughly chop the onions. Peel and finely chop the garlic. Wash the parsley, shake dry and roughly chop. Cut white cabbage into wide strips and wash. Peel the carrots and potatoes and cut into cubes. Also cut the bacon into cubes.

Leave the bacon cubes out in the hot pressure cooker. Steam the onion pieces in it until translucent, then add the meat and brown all over, sprinkle with garlic. Spread the carrots on top, season with salt and sprinkle with caraway seeds, then put a layer of cabbage on top and finally layer the potatoes, then sprinkle with salt and caraway seeds again. Heat the meat stock and pour in. Close the pressure cooker.

Cook for 25 minutes, then open the lid, mix everything together and season with salt and pepper.

PUT IN CHILI PEPPERS

Ingredients for 4 servings

- 600   G   Chili peppers
- 400   ml   water
- 300   ml   Vinegar (at least 5% acid)
- 2   Pc   Clove of garlic (cut into small pieces)
- 100   ml   Bona oil
- 100   G   Granulated sugar
- 1.5   TL   salt
- 1   Tbsp   Peppercorns

time

30 min. Total time 25 min preparation time 5 min.cooking & resting time

preparation

Wash the chili peppers and pat dry with kitchen paper. Sterilize the mason jar by simmering it in boiling hot water for a few minutes. Then let it air dry.

Then layer the chili peppers close together in the glass.

In a large saucepan, bring the water, vinegar, oil, salt, sugar, peppercorns and garlic to a boil. Let simmer for about 3 - 5 minutes.

Pour the preserving stock over the chili peppers into the mason jar. The glass must be made completely full.

Immediately seal the jar airtight, allow to cool and store in a cool place.

COLESLAW

Ingredients for 4 servings

- 350   G   White cabbage
- 3rd   Pc   Carrots
- 1   TL   salt
- 1   prize   pepper
- 1   TL   Caraway seed

Ingredients for the marinade

- 3rd   Tbsp   Bona oil
- 2   Tbsp   vinegar
- 1   prize   sugar
- 1   prize   salt
- 1   TL   Mustard medium hot

time

120 min. Total time 30 min preparation time 90 min.cooking & resting time

preparation

Clean and finely slice the white cabbage. Wash in a colander and drain. Peel the carrots and slice them into pens. Mix the cabbage and carrots, season with salt and stir well. Let it steep for 1 hour.

Mix the oil, vinegar, mustard, sugar, pepper and salt to a marinade.

Squeeze out the cabbage and carrots, discard the resulting liquid. Pour the marinade over the cabbage and carrots, mix well and sprinkle with caraway seeds. Let it steep for another 0.5 hour.

CARROT MUFFINS

Ingredients for 8 servings

- 220 G Carrots
- 3rd Pc Eggs
- 100 G Sugar, brown
- 0.5 TL cinnamon
- 80 G Ground hazelnuts
- 1 TL Baking powder, coated
- 80 G Flour
- 2 Tbsp Icing sugar

time

35 min. Total time 15 min preparation time 20 min.cooking & resting time

preparation

For the hearty carrot muffins, first scrape, wash and finely grate the carrots. Separate eggs into yolks and whites. Beat egg whites into snow.

Preheat the oven to 170 ° C. Grease the muffin tray, stir the egg yolks with sugar and 3 tablespoons of hot water to a creamy mixture and fold in the grated carrots.

Sift the flour into a bowl and mix with the cinnamon, hazelnuts and baking powder. Then stir into the carrot cream with a wooden spoon. Finally fold in the egg whites.

Spread the batter into the muffin troughs and bake in the oven on the middle shelf for 20 minutes.

Allow to cool, fall out of the mold and dust with icing sugar.

PUMPKIN SLICE

Ingredients for 4 servings

- 1 Pc pumpkin
- 1 prize Seasoned Salt
- 1 prize pepper
- 2 Pc Eggs

- 100 ml milk
- 1 Cup Breadcrumbs

time

30 min. Total time 15 min preparation time 15 min.cooking & resting time

preparation

Bring a saucepan of salted water to the boil, in the meantime peel the pumpkin, cut into wedges and remove the seeds.

Cut the pumpkin into finger-thick slices and for 2-4 minutes in salted water blanch, strain - quench in ice water.

Drain the pumpkin well on kitchen paper, season with herb salt and pepper on both sides. Beat the eggs with the milk, first turn the pumpkin slices in flour, then pull them through the egg mixture and finally turn them in breadcrumbs.

Heat oil two fingers wide in a pan, bake the pumpkin schnitzel on both sides until golden brown, drain on paper towels and serve while still hot.

ZUCCHINI CHIPS

Ingredients for 4 servings

- 1   kg   zucchini
- 4th   Tbsp   Bona olive oil
- 1   Pc   Onion (red)
- 1   Tbsp   Bona olive oil
- 1   prize   pepper
- 1   prize   salt

time

20 min. Total time 10 min preparation time 10 min. cooking & resting time

preparation

Wash the zucchini and cut into approx. 5mm thick slices and dry them well.

Peel and cut the onion into eighths.

Let a pan get very hot, fry the zucchini slices on both sides in 4 tablespoons of oil, remove from the pan and season with salt and pepper, in the same pan fry the onion eighth in 1 tablespoon of olive oil and mix with the zucchini chips.

TOMATO PASTE

Ingredients for 4 servings

- 1   kg   Tomatoes (very ripe)
- 15th G   salt

time

40 min. Total time 20 min preparation time 20 min.cooking & resting time

preparation

For the homemade tomato paste, lightly cut the top of the tomatoes crosswise and remove the existing greens at the same time.

Then briefly blanch the tomatoes in a saucepan with boiling water and then peel the tomatoes.

Now quarter, core and puree the tomatoes.

Then mix in the salt and bring to the boil in a saucepan and allow to thicken. After boiling it briefly, it can also be pressed through a fine sieve or cheesecloth, so that only the pulp is left.

Fill into suitable screw-top jars and close airtight.

POTATO CHEESE

Ingredients for 2 servings

- 4th   Pc   potato
- 1   Pc   onion
- 0.5   cups   Schärdinger Berghof sour cream
- 0.5   TL   Caraway seed
- 1   prize   pepper
- 1   prize   salt

time

30 min. Total time 10 min preparation time 20 min.cooking & resting time

preparation

Boil the potatoes, peel them and press them through the potato press.

Peel onions and cut them into fine pieces. Mix well with the potato mixture and sour cream.

Season to taste with salt, pepper and caraway seeds. Wash, finely chop and mix in the chives.

APPLE HORSERADISH

Ingredients for 1 serving

- 100   G   Horseradish
- 1   Pc   Apple
- 1   shot   Lemon juice
- 1   TL   sugar
- 1   shot   vinegar

time

10 min. Total time 10 min preparation time

preparation

Peel the washed apple and horseradish. Use a fine grater to grate the horseradish and then the apple in a bowl and mix well.

Flavor with a dash of vinegar, sugar and lemon juice and let it steep for an hour in the refrigerator.

MILLET

Ingredients for 4 servings

- 2   Cup   millet
- 1   Pc   Bay leaf
- 1   prize   salt
- 4th   Cup   water
- 1   Pc   Onion (small)
- 1   Tbsp   Bona oil

time

55 min. Total time 20 min preparation time 35 min.cooking & resting time

preparation

Wash the millet with hot water before preparing it. Chop the onion and let it turn translucent in a little sunflower oil.

Add the millet and fry a little too.

Pour water on, add the bay leaf and salt.

Let the millet simmer for 5 minutes and let it swell for another 30 minutes.

TROUT MILLER

Ingredients for 4 servings

- 4th   Pc   350 g trout
- 2   Tbsp   chopped parsley
- 4th   Tbsp   butter
- 1   shot   Bona oil
- 80   G   Crumbs
- 80   G   Flour
- 1   Pc   Lemon, juice
- 1   prize   salt
- 1   prize   pepper
- 1   prize   salt

time

40 min. Total time 40 min preparation time

preparation

Gutting trout (best done by the fishmonger). Season the trout inside and out with salt and pepper.

Heat some oil in a coated, heat-resistant pan, roll the fish first in breadcrumbs, then in flour and fry on both sides.

Slide into the preheated oven to 180 ° C, turn over after approx. 4 minutes and fry again until the skin is golden yellow and crispy.

Marinate the lettuce with vinegar, oil, salt and pepper.

Arrange the finished trout on plates. Add the butter, lemon juice, parsley and salt to the roast residue in the pan, let it froth briefly and add the trout.

CHIVES AND EGGS SPREAD

Ingredients for 2 servings

- 4th   Pc   Eggs, hard-boiled
- 1   Federation   chives
- 4th   Tbsp   Schärdinger Berghof sour cream
- 1   prize   Lovage salt
- 2   prize   pepper
- 2   prize   salt

time

15 min. Total time 15 min preparation time

preparation

Wash the chives, shake dry, sort and let dry on kitchen paper. Peel and chop the eggs. Cut the chives into the finest rolls.

Put the eggs, chives, sour cream, pepper, lovage salt and salt in a bowl and stir. Season again to taste and portion.

VIENNESE PASTA SALAD

Ingredients for 4 servings

- 300   G   wide ribbon noodles
- 300   G   boiled ham
- 2   Tbsp   Bona olive oil
- 6th   Pc   Eggs
- 160   G   young Gouda
- 2   Federation   chives
- 5   Pc   Cocktail tomatoes
- 2   Tbsp   Sunflower seeds
- 1   prize   pepper
- 1   prize   salt

Ingredients for the salad dressing

- 4th   Tbsp   Bona oil
- 2   Tbsp   Pumpkin seed oil
- 2   Tbsp   Apple Cider Vinegar
- 2   Tbsp   Pear juice
- 1   prize   pepper
- 1   prize   salt

time

35 min. Total time 15 min preparation time 20 min.cooking & resting time

preparation

Cook the pasta in plenty of salted water according to the instructions on the package, drain, rinse briefly and drain well.

Cut the ham into 1 1/2 cm squares, heat the olive oil and fry in the hot olive oil.

Whisk the eggs with a little salt, pour over them, put the lid on and let set over the lowest heat.

Cut the cheese into 1 cm wide strips, cut the chives into 1/2 cm long rolls. Cut the tomatoes into small cubes.

Roast sunflowers in a non-stick pan.

Let the cooked pancake slide out of the pan and cut into fine strips.

Mix with pasta, ham, cheese, paprika and sunflower seeds.

Mix in a marinade from sunflower oil, pumpkin seed oil, apple cider vinegar, pear juice, salt and pepper and fold in.

WRAPS WITH SALMON

Ingredients for 3 servings

- 3rd   Pc   wraps
- 0.5   cups   Schärdinger Berghof sour cream
- 200   G   cream cheese
- dill
- 250   G   Salmon (smoked)
- 1   prize   pepper
- 1   prize   salt

time

20 min. Total time 10 min preparation time 10 min.cooking & resting time

preparation

For the wraps with salmon, first mix the sour cream with the cream cheese. Wash and finely chop the dill, fold in and season with salt and pepper.

Now brush the wraps with it and cover with the salmon slices. Now roll up the wraps and put them in cling film in the refrigerator for about 10 minutes.

Before serving, cut the wraps into 3 cm thick slices.

www.ingramcontent.com/pod-product-compliance
Lightning Source LLC
Chambersburg PA
CBHW080613100526
44585CB00035B/2406